AUDUBON'S

Birds of America

POPULAR EDITION

THE MACMILLAN COMPANY
NEW YORK · BOSTON · CHICAGO
DALLAS · ATLANTA · SAN FRANCISCO

MACMILLAN AND CO., LIMITED
LONDON · BOMBAY · CALCUTTA
MADRAS · MELBOURNE

**THE MACMILLAN COMPANY
OF CANADA, LIMITED**
TORONTO

AUDUBON'S

Birds of America

Introduction and Descriptive Captions

by Ludlow Griscom

POPULAR EDITION

THE MACMILLAN COMPANY

New York: 1950

TABLE OF CONTENTS

HERONS and BITTERNS *(Ardeidae)*

WOOD IBISES *(Ciconiidae)*

IBISES and SPOONBILLS *(Threskiornithidae)*

FLAMINGOS *(Phoenicopteridae)*

SWANS, GEESE, SURFACE-FEEDING DUCKS, DIVING DUCKS, RUDDY DUCKS, and MERGANSERS *(Anatidae)*

VULTURES (Cathartidae)

KITES, SHORT WINGED HAWKS, BUZZARD HAWKS, EAGLES, and HARRIERS (Accipitridae)

[8]

OYSTER-CATCHERS *(Haematopodidae)*

PLOVERS, TURNSTONES and SURF BIRDS
    (Charadriidae)

WOODCOCK, SNIPE, SANDPIPERS, etc. *(Scolopacidae)*

AVOCET and STILTS *(Recurvirostridae)*

ROBINS, BLUEBIRDS, etc. *(Turdidae)*

GNATCATCHERS and KINGLETS *(Sylviidae)*

WAXWINGS *(Bombycillidae)*

SHRIKES *(Laniidae)*

VIREOS *(Vireonidae)*

WOOD WARBLERS *(Parulidae)*

MEADOWLARKS, BLACKBIRDS and ORIOLES
(Icteridae)

TANAGERS *(Thraupidae)*

GROSBEAKS, FINCHES, SPARROWS, and BUNTINGS *(Fringillidae)*

INTRODUCTION

BY LUDLOW GRISCOM

IT IS NOW almost a century since the death of John James Audubon (1785–1851). Not only has his reputation lasted, but if anything, his fame and renown have increased with the passage of time. It, perhaps, might be worth while to pause and enquire why this is so. He is a perpetual source of study, discussion and debate, and much ink has been spilled over whether his claim to fame was primarily as an ornithologist or an artist. In my opinion much of this debate is second rate or even trivial, and misses the major point.

Actually he was both, and it is an irrelevant detail to consider in which field he may have excelled, for the moment. Moreover, his biography, letters, and delineations of the American scenery and manners of his day have acquired increasing value and historical interest with the years, and make good reading for people with no knowledge of birds whatever. To my view his greatest claims to fame and glory were first, the versatility of his talents and gifts, and second that the completion of his main ambition, the original elephant folio of paintings of 435 species of American birds against overwhelming odds was a *tour de force,* of a kind which has never again been equalled in history.

It is perhaps trite to remark that men who accomplish a *tour de force* usually lead extraordinary lives, and display characteristics not possessed by the humdrum citizen. Audubon was no exception to this rule. The son of a French naval officer and a creole woman of Santo Domingo, he was probably illegitimate, but never admitted it. Howbeit, the father was a man of some sub-

[15]

stance, and young Audubon had a spoiled and petted boyhood on an estate in France, early developing both a talent for drawing, and a love of the outdoors, natural history and birds in particular, which he could not control, and which motivated his entire life.

When about seventeen years of age, he was sent to North America to take charge of a property near Philadelphia, and thenceforth adopted his new country wholeheartedly. Here he met and married Lucy Bakewell, and began a series of commercial ventures with his patrimony, which took him to Kentucky in 1808 and to New Orleans in 1812. As Audubon could not restrain himself from a continual hunting, shooting and drawing, all these ventures failed, until finally he had practically nothing left except a wife, gun, and the precious drawings of his beloved birds. By 1822 most people in the pioneer settlements from the Ohio to New Orleans regarded him as an incompetent madman.

In the meantime his dream, to publish a series of paintings of every North American bird, had been crystallizing, and he determined to devote his time, talents and energy to the attainment of this goal, no matter what the cost. He was encouraged by his devoted and unselfish wife, who believed in his genius and a final triumphant success. For years Audubon led a truly remarkable life. Supporting himself by painting, portraiture, and teaching drawing, separated from his wife for years at a time, in some incredible manner he always got where he wanted to go, and attained all his objectives. He solicited subscriptions to his great work in the principal eastern cities, going back and forth to Edinburg, London and Paris, most of the time leading a hand-to-mouth existence. In 1831 he made his famous expedition to the Florida Keys, the next year going to Labrador, then travelling through the southern states to the independent republic of Texas, always seeking out wilderness areas. In between trips he wrote the volumes of the text, and the whole work was completed in 1838 at a cost of about $100,000, the total number of sets issued being under two hundred, at $1,000 a set. The project had taken just about twenty-five years to complete, his wife's faith was justified, success and renown were his.

This success would have been impossible without the possession of qualities, many of which the world properly regards as magnificent. Audubon had enormous confidence in himself, inflexible determination, and the capacity of never admitting failure or becoming really discouraged. His physical endurance and energy were extraordinary, and some of his adventures required great bravery. His dealings with others were aided by a magnetic personality, he was remarkably handsome with beautiful eyes, and practised the arts of self-dramatization and salesmanship instinctively. The American Woodsman became a sensational success in the houses of the great and near great. Audubon's life has been described as a typical success story; he just could not be stopped.

Audubon's later life further illustrates his remarkable energy. In 1840 he began work on the octavo edition of his *Birds of America,* completing the text of the seven volumes in only four years, and taking time out for his last and most perilous expedition to the Great Plains and Rocky Mountains when he was nearly sixty. Moreover, shortly prior to 1846, he had completed all 155 paintings of the quadrupeds of North America. By the irony of fate his health and mind began to fail rapidly in 1848, and he became totally blind before he died in 1851.

In this book we are chiefly concerned with Audubon as an artist and ornithologist, and we pass to a critique of his stature in these two fields. There can be no question of his place as an artist. He is one of the American immortals, his originals are priceless, and only the very rich can afford the earlier octavo editions. It is high time that bird-lovers were reminded again of what Audubon set out to do and what his contribution was. Illustrations of birds prior to him were mostly incredibly crude. The artist drew the stuffed and mounted specimen, about which he knew nothing, often faithfully reproducing the unnatural lumps in the outline of the body, and foreshortening the neck and tail. The colors faithfully showed any fading or dirt on the mount, and little effort was made to indicate the fact that the bird's body was coated with feathers. Finally the bird was placed on a conventionalized perch or twig, not in the least resembling any twig existing in nature.

Audubon's paintings were life-sized portraits in natural attitudes, in a natural habitat, or perched on a flower or tree of a species actually existing and instantly recognizable. Only the well-informed ornithologist can criticize some of his work. He dramatized his birds as well as himself. The colors of some are too bright, the poses of others are too striking, or they are in startling attitudes which the bird actually never adopts in life. We happen to live in an age of extreme exactitude, bird portraits in color are hopelessly expensive, and the goal of most illustration today is scientific delineation, measured out to the last millimeter, as an aid to identification and recognition. Thus Audubon's Bald Eagle is easily seen to have eleven tail feathers, whereas eagles possess twelve. No modern illustrator of birds would dream of making so unimportant a slip, which of course in no way detracts from the artistic as well as lifelike effect.

If a sort of Gallup poll were held, and the question were asked— "Can you mention the name of some noted ornithologist?," it is my best guess that a substantial percentage of the better educated Americans would answer, "Audubon" without hesitation. It is equally my guess that only those with a special interest in birds would ever have heard of any other!

Various competent ornithologists have given critiques of Audubon, and have, quite fairly, pointed out his limitations. He did indeed discover many new birds, and he added greatly to our knowledge of many others, but he was not at all scientifically minded in technical directions, and made no effort to improve the classification of birds in the higher categories of genera and families. In many directions his artistic side dominated the scientific. The ornithologist who discovers and describes new birds, or who finds others in America for the first time, invariably prizes and preserves the specimen as a permanent voucher or proof of his discovery. To Audubon, the precious possession to which he clung no matter what the adversity of his circumstances, was his painting. Throughout most of his life he threw the specimens away after the painting was completed, never supposing that his integrity or fidelity to nature would be questioned. He has, therefore, left behind him a certain number of insoluble mysteries. On the one hand he claims to have seen or shot and painted some well known European birds, never seen or heard of in the New World again. On the other hand, he discovered, described and painted several "new" species, also never heard of again, none of which can be explained away as hybrids, freaks, or a plumage variation of any bird we know. Needless to say, in these last cases particularly, modern science would give anything to have the original specimen preserved and available for study. Finally, some of Audubon's "errors" were really due to the misinformation of friends and correspondents in whom he had confidence. Thus specimens of certain sea birds were sent him, purporting to come from the "mouth of the Columbia River" in Oregon, which actually were collected at Cape Horn, or near it.

Other criticisms of Audubon reflect chiefly on the critics. It is common sense that we have learned a lot about the birds of eastern North America since Audubon's day, and are still adding to knowledge about them. Moreover, every corner of a great continent has now been explored, half of which Audubon never penetrated, containing birds of whose existence he remained unaware. It is obviously no reflection on this remarkable man that there was plenty to find out after his death. Think of the handicaps and difficulties under which he labored, the difficulties of transportation and travel, the lack of field glasses, to mention only a few. We consequently find that his knowledge was most incomplete with the small forest and tree-top birds that he could not observe from the ground, and that he shot on a few occasions only by pure chance. In common with all early or pioneer ornithologists, he could not work out the relationships of technically very difficult groups of birds like the gulls, terns, small flycatchers and certain thrushes. His experience was inadequate to determine that some of his species were nothing but the immature or winter plumages of birds well known to him only in their adult plumages. He was unable to unravel the puzzling color phases of certain hawks. There is little merit in attempting to depreciate him because he did not know certain things that it took two generations of ornithologists after him to find out.

In spite of various things Audubon did not know about American birds, the passage of time has rendered some of the things he did know and some of the things he saw of ever increasing interest and historical value. He foretold the inevitable disappearance of the wilderness, and remarked on the rapid decrease of various birds in his own lifetime. Actually he could never have even conceived of the rapid acceleration of tempo with which scientific inventions have enabled our civilization to take possession of the country, exploit its natural resources, utterly change the landscape, and destroy the natural habitats which nature had provided. Never in history has a native continental fauna ever been called on to endure so sudden and catastrophic a change, and endeavor to survive. Added to this, a large list of birds suffered intense persecution from sport, market gunning, the plume trade, cage-bird traffic and other reasons. There were practically no game laws worthy of the name in the whole country, and they could not be enforced in unsettled regions. No sentiment of any kind in favor of most birds existed. Hawks, crows, owls, and all large water and marsh birds were natural targets for hunters and travellers on which to practise marksmanship. Small boys learned to shoot by popping away at the birds on the lawn. We must also remember that in Audubon's time even robins and blackbirds were regarded as game, while the poor gathered gulls' and terns' eggs for food.

The results can easily be appreciated. Several famous American birds are extinct. Two, the Labrador Duck and Great Auk, were little known even in Audubon's time, but the Carolina Paroquet

was common, and the Passenger Pigeon existed in such spectacular multitudes that it was one of the great wonders of the
living world. Several others are on the verge of extinction. The
game supply of the continent was decimated beyond recovery,
roughly speaking only about 10 per cent of it surviving into modern times. A large number of other birds greatly decreased by
reason of the destruction of the forests, the drainage of marshes,
and the spoiling of much country by civilization. Audubon has
left us accounts of these rare and vanished birds. The numbers of
some of the game birds he saw were so prodigious as to appear
incredible to the present generation of bird-lovers. Thus a two-
day October flight of woodcock down the Ohio River was esti-
mated by him to consist of between thirty and forty thousand.
It is problematical if any expert devoting himself to hunting this
bird could manage to see that many in a lifetime today.

One of the many points of interest about birds is a characteristic
which may loosely be termed "powers of adaptation." This is in
marked contrast to lower or less evolved groups of animals, as
well as the plants, which are the unconscious victims of blind
chance; these live or perish according to whether their circumstances are favorable or unfavorable. But most birds can take
some steps to mitigate or improve their lot. They can leave an
area where they are hunted, acquire wariness under persecution,
adopt new habitats, abandon their natural shyness and suspicion
upon learning that it is uncalled for. Birds put up with or even
adopt the vicinity of man if he does them no harm. In other words
they can adapt themselves to new or changed conditions, whether
for better or for worse.

American birds began adapting themselves to the changes
brought about by the white man in early colonial times. The
robin, swallows, chimney swift, and martin became familiar dooryard birds. Audubon took for granted that a great variety of
common birds were characteristic of gardens, orchards, fields and
pastures, without stopping to think that these habitats had never
previously existed. They were created by the white man delib-

erately, involving the destruction of the original primeval forest. This event serves to illustrate and explain a fundamental principle in natural history and biology. It is *impossible* to destroy one habitat without automatically creating another. The destruction of the forest may well involve the loss or disappearance of some or most of those birds and animals requiring it as a habitat, and we may well mourn their decrease or extinction. But some at least of these forest birds adapted themselves to the new conditions. The robin, for instance, was originally a forest bird, and still is in remote parts of the continent. The chimney swift nested in hollow trees in the forest before there were any chimneys.

It consequently follows that the changes brought about by the white man created a great boon for those birds requiring or preferring forest edges, sprout woods, thickets, and open country of every kind. At least one hundred species are now common, well known, and widely distributed, which were absent or else rare and local in most of the forested northern and eastern states in early colonial times. Our final debt to Audubon is that he left us some invaluable data on this subject. In certain cases he has told us what type of country a certain bird inhabited in his time, now found in radically different environments. Even more interesting are those cases, where the bird was rare and little known to him, but a species now common and widely distributed. Several warblers preferring second-growth woodlands will illustrate this category, and we have a definite historic record of their arrival in and gradual spread over much of the Northeast since Audubon's time.

Audubon's name has become indelibly associated with the popular movement to protect and conserve American birds. Some seventy years ago thoughtful and high class sportsmen, appalled at the increasingly rapid decimation of game, began to agitate for the absolute necessity for restrictive legislation. At this period practically no bird received any legal protection whatever. In a few states certain game birds had a brief closed season during most of or a part of their breeding season only, and there were virtually no bag limits whatever. Moreover, any method was legal, including the most destructive, such as night shooting, fire lighting, netting and trapping. The last great nesting flock of Passenger Pigeons in Michigan was so unmercifully raided that over one hundred million birds were shipped to city markets. Chesapeake Bay was a noted paradise for waterfowl. Market gunning began there in 1795, was pursued throughout the season (September 15–April 15) at a steadily increasing tempo, so that by 1870, up to fifteen thousand ducks were killed in a day. As the same activity was going on in every other locality where water-fowl were numerous, the decimation in numbers of this group of birds can be imagined. The plume trade reduced the egrets and most terns to the verge of extinction.

The various state, and, finally (1904) the National, Audubon societies were an outgrowth of the original bird protection committee of the American Ornithologists Union (1883). These societies were led by thoughtful sportsmen and ornithologists, but their rise to power, influence and adequate financing was chiefly due to the rise of popular interest in birds, which began about 1895 and has been going on ever since. The era of bird protection was rapidly and triumphantly successful. By 1920 every North American bird was protected, the federal government had taken over the control of all migratory birds, any form of commercial use of native birds was illegal, a large number of birds had been permanently removed from the game list, and the open season and permissible take on the remainder had been drastically reduced, and this reduction has still been going on. The results have been most gratifying. Over one hundred species of North American birds have greatly increased in numbers, and some are already as numerous as at any time in the historical period.

The one possible criticism the naturalist can make of the extensive literature of the bird protection era was its uniformly pessimistic tone. It was probably necessary for arousing a supine public, but was not entirely true. It was indeed very true that from 1850–1900 far more birds were rapidly decreasing than the few which were increasing. It is human nature to sigh for what has been lost, and to take what one has for granted. The other natural error of this era was the general belief that the rapid decrease of many birds was due wholly to overshooting.

This fallacy is now being gradually corrected by time and experience, but must still be sold to the vast number of Americans interested in birds. We now know that many of the birds completely protected for many years will *never* regain their former numbers, or anything anywhere near it. The reason is that our civilization has destroyed too large a percentage of their required habitat, and they lack the necessary powers of adaptation to adopt a new one or make some compromise. This leads to a second great general principle in natural history. The total number of existing individuals of any bird or animal can never be greater than the amount of favorable habitat existing or remaining, and the total amount of the necessary food.

We speak of marsh and water birds without stopping to think that they have to have marshes and water. Our civilization has drained millions of acres of marshland, and is continuing to do so at a rapid rate. Innumerable streams are polluted or dried up by a century of building operations. Ponds and lakes are now surrounded by cabins and camps, and covered with boats and canoes for parts of each year. For many water birds such a lake has become a total loss. It transpires that food cannot be taken for granted. The Brant Goose feeds on eel-grass almost exclusively, and was so seriously reduced when a disease struck this plant that it had to be removed from the game list for some years. The Ivory-billed Woodpecker is almost certainly about to become extinct in the near future, because highly specialized food habits require a substantial acreage of primeval forest to keep one pair alive. As civilization has eliminated the southern primeval forest, the few surviving individuals are doomed.

Along the lines of this exposition the era of bird protection passed rapidly but imperceptibly into the era of conservation. Our birds are protected, but still need to be conserved. The Golden

Age has not arrived because we have stopped shooting. Never are all of them prospering and doing well at any one time. Particularly hard pressed are our few remaining game birds, whose foes, the sporting fraternity, are increasing by leaps and bounds, as leisure, means, and facilities of transportation increase. But all the birds are being put under constant strain and difficulty by the multiple and rapid changes which an expanding technological civilization is making on the face of our land. Forest fires, lumbering, and oil wells ruin vast stretches of country yearly; the prairies are fenced in and overgrazed by cattle and sheep; intercoastal canals bring salt water into fresh water bays and landlocked sounds, ruining and disrupting the native plants and animals. Fields and pastures are plowed up and planted to corn or vegetables; some farmer's woodlot of last summer is cut down for firewood during the winter; every year some local marsh is used as a town dump and gradually filled in. Every one of these habitats supported a rich community of bird life. Where do they go?

Conservation consequently involves an intelligent and successful effort to preserve major habitats and types of country, in as natural a state as possible. Hence the great development of national and state parks, national and state forests, and the great chain of federal wild life refuges. A new profession of wild life management has arisen, an outlet for young naturalists. The refuge area must be maintained and guarded; it can also be improved. Dams can be built, artificial ponds can be created, the more desirable food plants can be introduced, and water levels preserved. The manager and his staff can count and note the increase in the wild life, observe the relative success of the breeding season. The plants, animals and birds requiring all these types of country are almost automatically conserved for the enjoyment of posterity. One good proof of the overall success of this movement is the steadily increasing number of campers, tourists and visitors, the money involved supporting a variety of industries in the economic sense. A forceful and able executive staff is also essential.

[25]

The appropriations must be secured from Congress, and above all the constant effort to raid the parks, forests, and refuges for other interests must be fought off. Our civilization is now so complex that it is almost impossible to do anything without hurting some one else's interest. The army and navy are looking for bombing ranges in wilderness areas, where there is no risk of blowing our citizens up. Power dams and major irrigation projects often threaten these areas. The ranchers seek grazing privileges in the parks and forests, the lumber interests are perpetually trying to get permission to cut down a tiny piece of some forest. Everlasting vigilance is required.

It follows that we live in a state of perpetual change and flux. As habitats are destroyed and replaced by others, one group of birds comes in and another goes out. Every decade some bird begins to fade out, some other bird learns to adapt itself to man, and begins to flourish and increase. The Duck Hawk or Peregrine Falcon is turning metropolitan. More and more spend much of the year in cities, roosting on a church spire or skyscraper, living on the city pigeons. The Snowy Owl from the arctic has also become a suburbanite, visiting the local dump nightly for rats. Everyone is glad to see them, and appreciates their service as vermin reducers. Every nature lover, every bird watcher, every member of the Audubon Society can now make a contribution. He can count and keep careful watch over his local birds, detect the upward and downward trends, and report them. The sum of the local reports equals the welfare of each species in its total range. Never in history have there been so many ways in which a bird-lover can find interesting and worth while things to do with his hobby. Any boy or girl of high school age can learn to identify their local birds and begin useful work.

There is one other major principle in natural history the understanding of which makes the pursuit of any branch of it more interesting. The real harm done by the white man and his civilization is his ruthless and wasteful exploitation of the rich natural resources of this continent. In so doing he has utterly upset and disrupted the balance of nature. The question arises just what is the balance of nature? We may begin with our birds, which require a suitable habitat and an adequate food supply. But birds are not the only living creatures in the habitat, and their food can only be other living animals and plants. Therefore the bird in its habitat is one member only of a living or natural community, and is dependent upon the other living members of the community. Actually the soil, water and climate are the basic factors. The plants come next, followed by insects, and last of all the birds and mammals. This succession is easily proved in areas devastated by a volcanic eruption, or where a great glacier has melted and retreated in a cycle of warmer climate. But complete interdependence exists among the living members of the community. There is a fascinating chain of interrelationships. The insects eat the plants, but they are essential in pollinating the flowers. The birds live in the trees and eat the insects. The foxes live on the mice, which live on the plants. The hawks live on the song birds. Everything is preyed upon by something, but everything also performs an essential service by keeping in check the numbers of something else. The balance of nature in a natural community is such that the community continues forever. This is accomplished by keeping the numbers of each living creature in a proper proportion. The foxes obviously never eat up *all* the mice, or they would exterminate themselves. As no living creature can afford to exterminate its food supply, the food supply is more abundant individually than its enemy or predator. Therefore there never are as many foxes as mice, or as many hawks as song birds, or as many insects as plants. Any increase in mice is sure to initiate an era of prosperity for foxes, which automatically causes the reduction of the mouse population to normal, which starves out the extra foxes. And so on *ad infinitum*.

The civilized white man is the only living creature who has the power to disrupt the balance of nature and exploit his food supply and natural resources without immediate, disastrous results. In America we have impoverished our soil, overgrazed our prairies, killed our game more rapidly than it can reproduce, and cut down our forests more rapidly than nature can replace them. This is easily seen to be stupid folly if we stop to think that our food-plant crops require fertile soil, and that our civilization absolutely requires timber and wood. Hence the modern efforts in money and talented man power to inculcate the principles of conservation before it is too late. And so we take one more backward glance at the great figure of Audubon, his vanished wilderness, and mourn the further loss and decrease of the many striking and spectacular birds he loved so well.

Audubon's original elephant folio of the *Birds of America* contained plates of 435 different birds. These were reproduced by The Macmillan Company in *The Birds of America* in royal octavo size, first published in 1937. The present work is designed to bring a selection of Audubon's paintings within the reach of all, so that everyone, even high school students, can get a glimpse of his decorative artistry and genius. The plates are consequently reduced to a more convenient size, and the total number has been cut from 435 to 288. Great care and thought have gone into this selection, and several factors have been given consideration. In the first place, virtually all species either erroneously recorded or mere vagrants and waifs to our shores have been omitted. In the second place all lost and mythical species have been left out, including those which are now known to be plumage stages or color phases of other species also painted by Audubon. In selecting from the remainder, two guiding principles have been adopted. Preference has been given to those paintings of superior merit and artistry, and the famous, more striking, and better known birds of America have been chosen rather than smaller and more inconspicuous ones, no matter how common. The book is designed for a much wider public than the small group of bird watchers with specialized knowledge and interest. Only this latter group is aware of a host of obscurely colored little sparrows, a variety of small sandpipers, gulls and warblers, the recognition of which involves years of technical study. The term "better known" is hereby used in a purely popular sense, and bears no connotation whatever as to the completeness of our scientific or ornithological knowledge. Numerous Americans have at least heard of our waterfowl and game birds, the more striking and conspicuous water birds such as pelicans and the flamingo, as well as a number of the smaller birds closely associated with and familiar to man, frequently mentioned in poetry and general literature. Hence the four most famous extinct birds of North America are included, so that people may know what they looked like, and it is regarded as of no consequence that no one can ever see them alive and use the plates as a means of identification.

The brief captions are consistent with the basic purpose of the book and the selection of paintings and continue one of the themes in the introduction. Limitations of space compel the omission of the scientific or technical name, any attempt to describe the nest, eggs and song, or any discussion as to method of identification or recognition in life. This last point is feasible and profitable only when *every* species of a closely related group is shown. Then only is there a basis for comparison and contrast. The main body of the caption gives some general idea of the preferred habitat or type of country in which the bird is found, followed by a general approximation of its range, that part of the United States in which it occurs. The extreme brevity adopted requires some explanation here. From the standpoint of bird distribution North America may be divided into three principal zones, 1) the treeless arctic; 2) the boreal coniferous forest stretching across the continent, extending south to the extreme northern states, and still farther south in the mountains at increasing altitudes; 3) a warmer temperate zone embracing most of the United States and parts of extreme southern Canada. This last zone has three well marked longitudinal sections, 1) an eastern forested section, 2) a central belt of great plains and prairies, 3) a western, much drier and mountainous forested area from the eastern base of the Rocky Mountains to the Pacific.

The reader is urged to remember that most North American

birds are highly migratory. They leave relatively northern breeding grounds and pass southward to often remote and far distant winter quarters. In such cases it is left to the common sense of the reader to deduce that in the intermediate geographic area these birds occur only during a brief period each spring and fall. In line with the conservation theme in this introduction some indication is given of whether each bird is rare, common, or abundant. Without fail, any marked change in status or numbers since Audubon's time is mentioned. Audubon's pictures were mostly life-sized, and when reduced and reproduced, no means are left for guessing that a bird on one plate may be ten times as large as the figure on some other plate. Each caption closes, therefore, with some figures to indicate the bird's total length, in inches, and the wing spread is given if particularly impressive.

Audubon's paintings of birds were published in a purely haphazard order, perhaps mainly the one in which he happened to complete them. The 288 here selected have been arranged in scientific order as being both more useful and informative. The various birds are, therefore, grouped together in the families in which they belong, and the sequence of families follows the accepted order currently in vogue. A table of contents gives the technical names of these families, as well as the common names, and next comes the species selected in each.

AUDUBON'S
Birds of America

1. COMMON LOON

Breeds on lakes from Alaska and Labrador to New England, North Dakota and California. Winters south to Florida and the Gulf coast, chiefly on larger lakes and coastal salt water. Quite common. Length 28-36 inches.

2. HOLBOELL'S GREBE

Breeds on lakes in Canada and northern tier of states from Minnesota westward. Winters chiefly on salt water on both coasts. Uncommon and reduced in numbers, now once more increasing. Length 18-20 inches.

3. HORNED GREBE

Breeds in lakes across Canada south to extreme northern United States. Winters chiefly on salt water on both coasts and the Gulf. Very common. The plate shows both summer and winter plumage. Length 13-15 inches.

4. EARED GREBE

Breeds in lakes from southern Canada and the Great Plains states westward. In winter on salt water on Pacific coast, and south to lakes of Mexico. Quite common. Both plumages shown. Length 12-14 inches.

5. PIED-BILLED GREBE

Breeds locally in ponds and lakes throughout most of New World from
southern Canada southward, retiring from the north in winter. Very
common. Rare on salt water. Known as hell-diver. Length 12-15 inches.

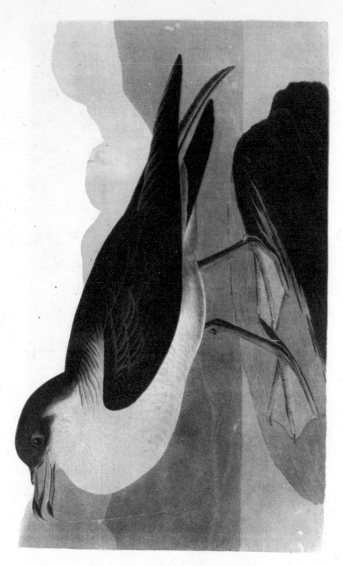

6. GREATER SHEARWATER

A bird of far southern latitudes, spending its winter in the North
Atlantic, hence a summer visitor. Oceanic, spending its time gliding
over the open ocean looking for food. Rarely seen from land. Length
18-20 inches.

7. LEACH'S PETREL

Breeds in burrows on small islands in the North Atlantic and Pacific, spending most of its life over the ocean far from land, and migrating far southward. Note the forked tail. Length 8 inches.

8. WILSON'S PETREL

A summer visitor on the North Atlantic, from far southern latitudes.
Very common, occasionally entering bays, sounds, and harbors. Note
rounded tail and yellow feet. Length 7 inches.

9. YELLOW-BILLED TROPIC-BIRD

A striking sea-bird of tropical oceans, nesting on lonely islets, north to Bermuda. Occasionally off the coast of the eastern states after hurricanes, chiefly southward. Dives from a height. Length 19 inches with tail streamers.

10. BROWN PELICAN

A bird of warm coastal waters from North Carolina and California to northern South America. Common and striking, diving with a great splash for fish which they carry in a huge throat pouch. Length 45-54 inches.

11. WHITE PELICAN

A few known nesting colonies on lakes in the far West and Northwest, migrating to the Gulf coast and Florida. One of the most superb of American birds, now happily increasing once more. Length 55-70 inches; wing spread 6½ feet.

12. GANNET

A striking sea bird, nesting in a few colonies on cliffs in the North
Atlantic; south to Florida in the winter. Dives from a great height.
Rapidly increasing. Plate shows immature and adult plumage. Length
34-40 inches.

13. EUROPEAN CORMORANT

In America from Greenland to the Gulf of St. Lawrence, south in winter to Massachusetts and Long Island, preferring rocky sea coasts. Greatly reduced, now rapidly increasing. Length 34-40 inches.

14. DOUBLE-CRESTED CORMORANT

Locally throughout most of North America on coastal cliffs and islets, and inland on lake borders and swamps, retiring southward in winter. Formerly greatly reduced in the East, now rapidly increasing, and extending its range. Length 30-35 inches.

15. WATER-TURKEY; SNAKE-BIRD

Southern cypress swamps and rice marshes south through tropical
America. Local and uncommon. Note the long, thin neck, the long
fan-shaped tail, and the brownish immature. Length 34 inches.

16. MAN-O'-WAR BIRD; FRIGATE BIRD

Tropical coasts north to Florida and southern Texas. A scavenger, unable to dive, and soaring magnificently on slender wings. Occasionally numerous after hurricanes. Length 40 inches; wing spread 7½ feet.

17. GREAT WHITE HERON

Extreme south Florida and the Keys, reduced by civilization and hurricanes to a few hundred individuals. Now protected and increasing. Note the yellow legs. Hybridizes with the Great Blue. Length 4½ feet.

18. GREAT BLUE HERON

Breeds locally from Alaska and southern Canada throughout the continent to Mexico, retiring southward in winter. Quite common, and increasing in recent years with protection. Length 42-52 inches.

19. AMERICAN EGRET

Breeds from Oregon, Minnesota and New Jersey southward. The plume trade reduced it to the verge of extinction. Now once more common and extending its range. Note black legs. Length 37-40 inches.

20. SNOWY EGRET

Range about the same as the last. Even more reduced by the plume trade. While common once more in the South, it has not yet recaptured its range in Audubon's time. Note black and yellow bill, legs and feet. Length 20-27 inches.

21. REDDISH EGRET

Now surviving only in south Florida and coastal Texas, slowly increasing with protection. Also in Cuba and on both coasts of Mexico. Note carefully the color of bill and legs. Length 29 inches.

22. LOUISIANA HERON

From New Jersey and Gulf coast of Texas far southward. Very common, increasing, and extending its range. Of slender and graceful shape, with a white rump and belly. Length 26 inches.

23. LITTLE BLUE HERON

Range about the same as last. Always common, now abundant. The white young birds are recognized by the color of bill and legs. All these herons wander north in late summer. Length 20-29 inches.

24. GREEN HERON

Breeds locally throughout the country north to southern Canada, retiring southward in winter. Not as colonial and gregarious as the larger herons, and rarely seen in any numbers. Length 16-22 inches.

25. BLACK-CROWNED NIGHT HERON

Southern Canada south throughout the country. Erratically distributed;
common in one section, rare and local in another, absent in a third.
Rapidly increasing in the Northeast since persecution ceased. Length
23-28 inches.

26. YELLOW-CROWNED NIGHT HERON

Eastern states from Long Island and Illinois southward. Uncommon and inexplicably local. Secretive and nocturnal. Rapidly increasing and extending its range in recent years. Length 22-28 inches.

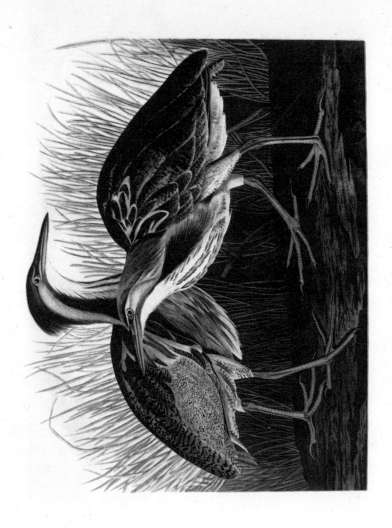

27. AMERICAN BITTERN

A secretive heron of marshes and swamps from southern Canada southward. Famous for its pumping noises, caused by forcing air from the
air sacs in the throat and neck. Length 23-34 inches.

28. LEAST BITTERN

A tiny, secretive heron of marshes and swamps, difficult to see and hear. It breeds locally and uncommonly in the eastern states and the Pacific coast, retiring well south in winter. Length 11-14 inches.

29. WOOD IBIS

The only North American stork. From Texas and South Carolina to tropical America. Local and uncommon, chiefly in coastal swamps. A spectacular bird, often soaring in large flocks. Length 35-47 inches.

30. WHITE IBIS

Swamps of the southern states southward. Tending to gather in huge
rookeries, where food is abundant; hence local and shifting about.
The great flocks are most impressive. Length 22-27 inches.

31. SCARLET IBIS

Chiefly northern South America, straggling to the southern states after hurricanes. Said to be rapidly decreasing. One of the most gorgeous and spectacular birds of the world. Length 22-27 inches.

[63]

32. GLOSSY IBIS

Exceedingly rare and local. Reduced to a few thousand birds in south Florida, Cuba, and possibly Louisiana. A spectacular bird, given to erratic wandering in spring far northward. Length 22-25 inches.

33. ROSEATE SPOONBILL

Local colonies in Texas, Louisiana, and south Florida. Sadly reduced,
but increasing slowly with protection. A showy and spectacular bird.
Also in tropical America. Length 32 inches.

34. FLAMINGO

A few colonies known, West Indies, northern South America, Yucatan, and Galapagos Islands. Seriously reduced. Formerly of occasional occurrence on the Florida Keys, now accidental. Length 45 inches.

35. WHISTLING SWAN

Breeds in arctic America, wintering on a few favorable sounds and lakes on both coasts. Sadly reduced, but numbers about doubled in recent decades. Length 48-55 inches.

36. CANADA GOOSE

Breeds over whole of North America, south very locally to certain northern and western states, where it is increasing on wild life refuges. Still common and well known. Length 25-43 inches.

37. BRANT

Breeds in the high Arctic, wintering on both coasts in salt water sounds
and bays. Far too dependent upon eel grass for food, and decimated
when this plant is killed off. Length 23-30 inches.

38. WHITE-FRONTED GOOSE

Breeds in the Arctic, wintering locally from the Pacific to the Gulf coast west of the Mississippi. It prefers wet prairies and marshes, a shrinking habitat. The total number of birds is small. Length 27-30 inches.

39. SNOW GOOSE AND BLUE GOOSE

Breed in the Arctic. One small population winters on the Atlantic coast. Several million winter on the Gulf coast marshes and interior valleys of California and Mexico. The Blue Goose predominates in Louisiana, and is possibly a color phase. Length 25-38 inches.

40. MALLARD

The most abundant fresh water duck of the Northern Hemisphere, the
ancestor of all domestic varieties. It is rare or absent only in the Northeast. Length 20-28 inches.

41. BLACK DUCK

Confined originally to eastern North America from Labrador southward, but spreading westward in recent decades, and has now reached
North Dakota. Very common. Length 21-25 inches.

42. GADWALL

Breeding commonly from the Great Plains westward, wintering south to the Gulf coast and Mexico. Rare on the Atlantic coast, where it had begun to breed locally in recent years. Length 19-21 inches.

43. PINTAIL

Next to the Mallard the most abundant duck of the Northern Hemisphere. Formerly rare in the Northeast, but rapidly increasing in recent years. Length 26-30 inches.

[75]

44. GREEN-WINGED TEAL

Breeds in the northern half and winters in the southern portion of the
Continent. Rapidly increasing in the Northeast in recent years, where
it became rare a century ago. Common. Length 13-15½ inches.

45. BLUE-WINGED TEAL

More southerly in breeding range than the last, south to tropical
America in winter. Rare or lacking in western United States. Greatly
reduced in the Northeast, now rapidly increasing. Quite common.
Length 15-16 inches.

46. BALDPATE; AMERICAN WIDGEON

Breeding in northern America, wintering in southern states and Mexico. Absent as a breeding bird northeastward, and uncommon on the Atlantic coast north of Virginia. Length 18-20 inches.

47. SHOVELLER; SPOONBILL

From southern Canada southward, chiefly west of the Alleghenies.
Rare on migration in the Northeast, and uncommon on the whole
Atlantic seaboard. The bill is used as a mud strainer. Length 17-20
inches.

48. WOOD DUCK

Nesting in holes in wooded swamps in southern Canada and the eastern states, locally in the Northwest. Seriously reduced; now once more common with special protection. Length 17-20 inches.

49. CANVAS-BACK

Breeds in western United States and central Canada. Winters south-
ward on brackish bays and sounds. Rare or absent in the Northeast.
Sadly reduced in the last century. The most famous game duck of
America. Length 20-24 inches.

50. LESSER SCAUP DUCK

Breeds chiefly in Canada east of Hudson Bay. In winter to southern
states and tropical America. Rare or absent in the Northeast. The
Greater Scaup is closely similar but larger, and more northern in range.
Both species common. Length 15-18 inches.

51. AMERICAN GOLDEN-EYE

Breeding on wooded lakes and ponds from tree-line to the northern states. Wintering freely on salt water from the northern states to the Gulf. A hardy and abundant duck. Length 17-23 inches.

52. BUFFLEHEAD

Breeds in hollow trees chiefly in lakes in western Canada, formerly farther south and east. South in winter to the Gulf and on salt water on both coasts. Greatly reduced. Length 13-15 inches.

53. HARLEQUIN DUCK

Common in the northwest Pacific, south locally in western mountain
lakes. A rare bird in Labrador and Newfoundland, south to Long
Island, N. Y. In winter a bird of the surf off cliffs and rocky islands.
Length 15-17½ inches.

54. LABRADOR DUCK

Became extinct just after Audubon's time for unknown causes. Bred possibly in the Labrador peninsula, and wintered at sea on sandy shoals off the North Atlantic coast. Length 20-24 inches.

55. COMMON EIDER

The most oceanic of ducks breeding on islands from the Arctic to
Maine, and wintering about shoals often far from land. Resident in
the Northwest Pacific and Hudson Bay. Common. Length 22-26
inches.

56. KING EIDER

High Arctic in breeding range. Resident in the northwest, a few birds reaching the Great Lakes and the North Atlantic coast in winter. Length 21-24 inches.

57. STELLER'S EIDER

A peculiar and remarkably colored sea duck of eastern Siberia and the northwestern Arctic, a few reaching arctic Europe in winter, the majority in the Aleutian Islands. Length 16-20 inches.

58. WHITE-WINGED SCOTER

Breeds in Canada south to North Dakota. Winters on both coasts south to Mexico and Florida. In spectacular abundance on certain North Atlantic shoals. Length 20-23 inches.

59. SURF SCOTER

Breeds in arctic western Canada. Common on both coasts in winter.
Slightly earlier on migration than the last and a little less hardy.
Length 18-22 inches.

60. AMERICAN SCOTER

Breeds in arctic Canada, wintering on both coasts like the last two. The least common of the scoters, it numbers only 10 per cent of either of the last two. Length 17-21 inches.

61. RUDDY DUCK

Breeding in the west from southern Canada to California, rarely farther east. Wintering in lakes and coastal bays south to the Gulf.
Greatly reduced in the East, now increasing. Length 14-17 inches.

62. AMERICAN MERGANSER; GOOSANDER

Breeds on lakes in Canada and the northern states south to California in the mountains. Wintering chiefly on fresh water in most of the United States. Common and increasing. Length 22-27 inches.

63. RED-BREASTED MERGANSER; SHELLDRAKE

Breeds from the Arctic to some northern states. Winters chiefly on salt water on all coasts of United States. Rare on fresh water on migration. Abundant. Length 20-25 inches.

64. CALIFORNIA CONDOR

Formerly Pacific coast ranges from Oregon to Lower California. Some 70 individuals survive in mountain canyons of central California, where everything is being done to protect them. Immense; wing spread 10 feet.

65. TURKEY VULTURE

Most of United States and southern Canada, retiring southward in winter. A carrion feeder, a master at soaring in search of food. Has spread slightly northward in the East recently. Length 30 inches; wing spread 6 feet.

66. BLACK VULTURE

More southern than the last, absent from the Rocky Mountains westward. Has spread northward recently to Virginia and Maryland. Both vultures occur in the tropics. Length 24 inches; wing spread under 5 feet.

67. WHITE-TAILED KITE

A rare and beautiful hawk now almost extinct in the Southeast, a few
in Texas and California. Reappears in southern South America. Length
15½ inches.

68. SWALLOW-TAILED KITE

Another vanishing hawk, now found in river swamps in a few southeastern states. Formerly common and ranging much farther north.
Migrates to tropical America, where the species is resident and common. Length 24 inches.

69. MISSISSIPPI KITE

Rare and local in the southern states from South Carolina and Kansas southward. Migrates to Mexico. Now common only in parts of Texas and Oklahoma. Length 14 inches.

70. GOSHAWK

Boreal forests south to New England and the western high mountain
states. Given to southward winter irruptions when its food supply of
game birds and rabbits fails. Uncommon. Length 20-26 inches.

71. SHARP-SHINNED HAWK

Breeds from tree limit to the Gulf coast and the mountains of Mexico.
Highly migratory northward. Feeds on small birds. Very common.
Length 10-14 inches.

72. HARRIS'S HAWK

A species of savannahs in tropical America, ranging north to California,
the coastal prairies of Texas (where common) and western Louisiana.
Length 17-20 inches.

73. RED-TAILED HAWK

Breeds in woods from Alaska and Newfoundland southward. Retiring
southward in winter. Common. Very variable; albinistic, melanistic
and erythristic races and individuals are numerous. Length 19-25
inches.

74. RED-SHOULDERED HAWK

A hawk of rich lowland woods in southern Canada and the eastern
states, reappearing in valleys in California. Very common and increasing; adopting the wrecked wood lots near civilization. Length 18-24
inches.

75. BROAD-WINGED HAWK

Breeds commonly in mountain woods in southern Canada and the northern states, much more locally southward. Highly migratory, often in great flocks, many birds going to tropical America. Length 14-18½ inches.

76. ROUGH-LEGGED HAWK

Breeding in the Arctic, wintering from the Canada line to the central states, rarely farther. Very variable; the plate shows the light or normal phase, but a black phase is common. Length 20-23½ inches.

77. GOLDEN EAGLE

Mountains of Canada north to tree-line and common in the western mountain states. Rare and local in the East, where it was nearly exterminated. Wandering in winter to sea level. Length 30-40 inches; wing spread 6½-7½ feet.

78. BALD EAGLE ADULT

From tree-line to Florida, Texas and Lower California. Chiefly on both
coasts, large rivers, and lakes, hence local or a rare wanderer in many
sections. Primarily a robber and carrion feeder. Length 30-40 inches.

79. BALD EAGLE IMMATURE

Very variable in color. Some birds uniformly blackish; others variously
spotted or marked with white blotches. It takes 3-5 years to attain
the adult plumage, and all stages of transition occur.

80. MARSH HAWK

Nesting in meadows and swamps from central Canada southward.
Inhabiting all types of open country at other seasons. Pure grey males
are relatively scarce, for so common a hawk. Length 18-24 inches.

81. FISH HAWK

Breeds near water from Alaska and Labrador southward. Migrating
to tropical America. Locally common. Feeds entirely on fish, which it
catches by diving. Often robbed by the Bald Eagle. Length 21-24
inches; wing spread 4½-6 feet.

82. AUDUBON'S CARACARA

A species of tropical America, common on the prairies of coastal Texas, and locally on the prairies of central Florida, where it is protected by Audubon wardens. Length 22 inches.

83. GYRFALCON, BLACK PHASE

An arctic hawk of the whole Northern Hemisphere, rarely seen in winter in the northern states. The black phase predominates in southern Greenland and Labrador. Length 20-24 inches.

84. GYRFALCON, WHITE PHASE

This beautiful color phase predominates in Greenland and very rarely
reaches the United States. There is also a grey phase, which predominates in western America and Siberia.

85. DUCK HAWK; PEREGRINE FALCON

Locally on cliffs almost throughout the Continent. Northern birds are
highly migratory, and many use the coast line. One of the most swift
and powerful fliers. Length 15-20 inches.

86. SPARROW HAWK

From central Canada south over most of the New World. Highly migratory northward. Prefers open country, and has recently adapted itself to cities and suburban areas. Nests in holes. Length 9-12 inches.

87. SPRUCE GROUSE

Boreal evergreen forests of the Continent. Tame and stupid to a degree, it is greatly reduced southward, and is now rare and local in the United States. Length 15-17 inches.

88. RUFFED GROUSE

Resident in woodlands over the southern half of Canada and the whole United States north of the southern lowlands. A famous game bird, foolish and tame in the wilderness. Length 16-19 inches.

89. WILLOW PTARMIGAN

Resident over the whole American Arctic south to Newfoundland. The bird turns pure white in winter except for some black tail feathers. Length 15-17 inches.

90. TWO PTARMIGAN

1. The Rock Ptarmigan is high Arctic, differing from the last in having
a small, slender bill. 2. The White-tailed Ptarmigan lives above tree-
line in western mountain ranges from Alaska to New Mexico. Length
15-17 inches.

91. PRAIRIE CHICKEN

Prairies and plains from southern Canada to coastal Texas. Greatly reduced and largely extirpated eastward. Famous for its "booming" noises and dancing grounds. Length 18 inches.

92. SAGE GROUSE

Sagebrush plains of the western states and southern Canada. Now greatly reduced in numbers and very local. Length 20-28 inches.

93. SHARP-TAILED GROUSE

Open woodlands and prairie thickets from near tree-line to the northern prairie states. Greatly reduced and locally extirpated southward
and eastward. Length 17½ inches.

94. BOB-WHITE

From Mexico and Cuba north to southern Canada, mostly east of the Great Plains. Greatly reduced northward by the introduction of southern, non-hardy stock. Prefers open farming country. Length 8½-10½ inches.

95. VALLEY QUAIL

Pacific states from Oregon to Lower California in farms, gardens, desert scrub and even city parks. Well adapted to civilization and quite common. Length 10 inches.

96. WILD TURKEY GOBBLER

Rich southern woodlands from Pennsylvania to Florida; also coastal
Texas, and mountain canyons of Arizona south to Mexico. Extirpated
in the Northeast and some of the central states. Length 48 inches.

97. WILD TURKEY HEN

The turkey now shows distinct signs of increasing in parts of its range.
The domestic breeds with grey tails came originally from Mexico.
They escape and mingle with the wild birds. Length 36 inches.

98. WHOOPING CRANE

A magnificent bird, formerly common in the prairies of Canada and the central states, migrating to the Gulf and the Atlantic coast from New Jersey to Florida. Nearly extinct, some 30 birds surviving. Length 4½ feet.

99. SANDHILL CRANE

Arctic tundra and wet prairies, south very locally in the northern and
western states, wintering in California and Texas. Also in Florida and
south Georgia. Greatly reduced in the East. Length 40-48 inches.

100. LIMPKIN

A bird of tropical American marshes, very local and decreasing in Florida and south Georgia. Famous for its loud wailing cries at night. Called Courlan or Crying Bird. Length 28 inches.

101. KING RAIL

Breeds in swamps and fresh water marshes east of the Great Plains from extreme southern Canada and New England south to the Gulf, retiring southward in winter. Fairly common in the South; rare, local and secretive in the Northeast. Length 15-19 inches.

102. CLAPPER RAIL

Salt marshes of Atlantic and Gulf coasts north to southern New England; also on the coast of California. Common, except at its northern limits, where it is migratory. Very noisy. Length 14-16 inches.

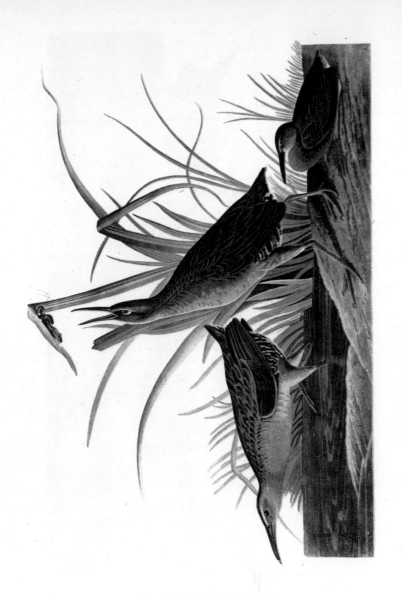

103. VIRGINIA RAIL

Widely distributed in marshes and swamps throughout the United States and southern Canada, but very local in arid areas. Secretive like all rails; best located by listening for its calls. Length 9-10½ inches.

104. SORA; CAROLINA RAIL

Of slightly more northern breeding range than the last, retiring to the
southern states with its relatives in winter. The most numerous of our
rails, often abundant in fall in rice marshes. Length 8-9¾ inches.

105. LITTLE BLACK RAIL

Rare and imperfectly known, about as hard to observe as a field mouse. Has been found in various states east of the Great Plains, and in coastal southern California. Length 5-6 inches.

106. FLORIDA GALLINULE

Widely scattered but very local throughout the United States, and also in many other parts of the world. Prefers marshes and swamps with deeper water, as it swims readily. Length 12-14½ inches.

107. AMERICAN COOT

An abundant bird throughout most of southern Canada and the United States, but very local in the breeding season. Gathers in great flocks on open lakes and brackish sounds in winter, diving for food like a duck. Length 13-16 inches.

108. OYSTER-CATCHER

Exceedingly local and uncommon, on sandy beaches from Maryland to Texas. Greatly reduced in numbers; in Audubon's time ranging north to Labrador. In other parts of the world also. Length 17-21 inches.

109. BLACK OYSTER-CATCHER

Pacific coast from southern Alaska to Lower California. Prefers rocky
shores and reefs, and still fairly common. Length 17-21 inches.

110. PIPING PLOVER

Sandy beaches of the Atlantic coast from Newfoundland to North Carolina; very locally on lakes and river bars in the interior. Winters in the South. Greatly reduced, now rapidly increasing. Length 6-7½ inches.

111. RING-NECKED PLOVER

Breeds in the Arctic, wintering from the southern states far southward.
In great abundance on both coasts on migration, a few in favorable
muddy habitats inland. Length 6½-8 inches.

112. WILSON'S PLOVER

Coastal sandy beaches from Maryland and California southward.
Greatly reduced, once more increasing. Note the long, stout, black
bill. Length 7-8 inches.

113. KILLDEER

Breeds in fields, pastures and plains throughout southern Canada and the United States. Abundant, noisy and conspicuous. Once more common in the Northeast, where it was nearly extirpated. Length 9-11 inches.

114. MOUNTAIN PLOVER

Rare and local in mountain prairies, plains and hillsides in a few
Rocky Mountain states. The few individuals in existence winter in
Texas, Mexico and interior California. Length 9 inches.

115. GOLDEN PLOVER

Arctic regions, migrating far southward. Once more abundant on the Atlantic coast, in smaller numbers on the Pacific coast, very few in now increasing rapidly. Length 10-11 inches.

116. BLACK-BELLIED PLOVER

Arctic regions, migrating to all southern continents. Now once more
abundant on both coasts of the United States, a few birds inland, and
wintering north to the central states. Length 10½-13½ inches.

117. RUDDY TURNSTONE

Arctic regions, migrating far southward. Once more abundant on the
Atlantic coast, in smaller numbers on the Pacific coast, very few in
the interior. Length 8-9½ inches.

118. SURF BIRD

Breeds in the high mountains of Alaska, migrating along the Pacific coast to Chile. Prefers the surf line on rocky coasts, and relatively uncommon. Length 11 inches.

119. WOODCOCK

A nocturnal, owl-like snipe of wooded swamps and wet thickets, breeding in southern Canada and the northern states east of the Plains, wintering in the South. Pathetically reduced since Audubon's time. Length 10-12 inches.

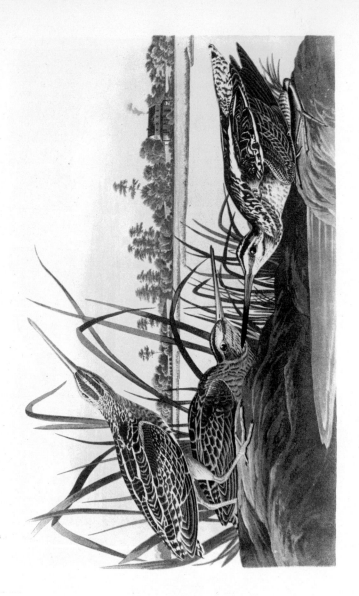

120. WILSON'S SNIPE

A bird of fresh-water marshes, bogs, and meadows, breeding in the
northern half of North America, wintering in the southern states and
tropical America. Greatly reduced in the East. Length 10½-11½ inches.

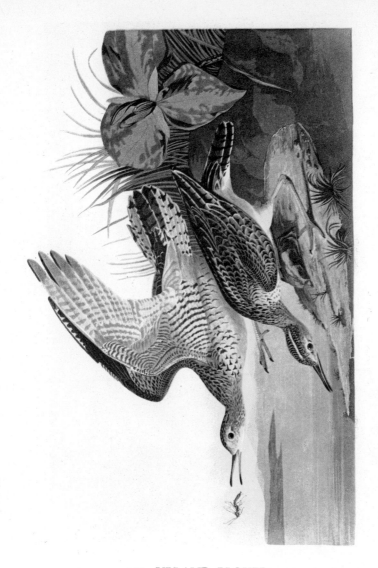

121. UPLAND PLOVER

Breeding in Alaska, Canada and the northern states in mountain
meadows, plains, prairies and pastures. Winters in southern South
America. Greatly reduced, now rare and local in the East. Length
11-12½ inches.

122. SPOTTED SANDPIPER

Throughout the country south of tree-line, migrating to tropical America. Common on all ponds, lakes and streams inland, as well as the
coast. Not gregarious like most shore birds. Length 7-8 inches.

123. SOLITARY SANDPIPER

Breeding in the Canadian wilderness, migrating to the tropics. An inland, fresh water sandpiper, casual on salt water. Lays its eggs in abandoned nests of other birds in trees. Length 7½-9 inches.

124. WILLET

Coastal marshes from Nova Scotia to Texas, very locally in the interior
and some western states. Retiring to the southern states and southward
in winter. Greatly reduced in the Northeast. Length 14-17 inches.

125. GREATER YELLOWLEGS

Arctic America, migrating far southward, a few wintering in the southern states. Abundant and well known on inland mud flats and margins as well as both coasts. Length 13-15 inches.

126. LESSER YELLOWLEGS

Range and habitat exactly as in the last, but a little more southerly in winter. Equally abundant. Differs from the last only in size and the readily distinguishable call notes. Length 9½-11 inches.

127. KNOT; ROBIN SNIPE

Arctic America, migrating far southward. Common on the Atlantic coast, uncommon on the Pacific, rarely alighting inland. Greatly reduced by market gunning, and not yet restored to its former abundance. Length 10-11 inches.

128. PURPLE SANDPIPER

Arctic America, south in winter to the northern coastal states. A bird of rocky reefs and coastal islets, casual on sandy beaches. The Atlantic population has recently adopted jetties and breakwaters. Length 8-9½ inches.

129. LEAST SANDPIPER

Breeding in the North, migrating to the tropics throughout the Continent, in interior fresh-water localities as well as both coasts. Abundant only east of the Rocky Mountains. Length 5-6½ inches.

130. RED-BACKED SANDPIPER; DUNLIN

Arctic America, south in winter to the southern states, wintering north
to Massachusetts. A relatively late migrant, now once more abundant
on the Atlantic coast. Less common on the Pacific, uncommon in
the interior. Length 8-9 inches.

131. DOWITCHER

Arctic America, migrating to the tropics throughout the Continent.
Once more abundant on both coasts, in smaller numbers in the interior.
Length 11-12½ inches.

132. STILT SANDPIPER

Arctic America, migrating to southern South America. Passing chiefly through the interior plains and prairies in the spring, a few on the Atlantic coast in fall. A very small total population. Length 7½-9 inches.

133. SEMIPALMATED SANDPIPER

Arctic America, migrating to the tropics. The most abundant small
sandpiper throughout the country, some in fresh-water inland localities.
Length 5½-6½ inches.

134. BUFF-BREASTED SANDPIPER

Arctic America, migrating to southern South America. A rare and sadly reduced sandpiper of the coastal prairies and Great Plains, a few eastward in fall. Length 7½-8½ inches.

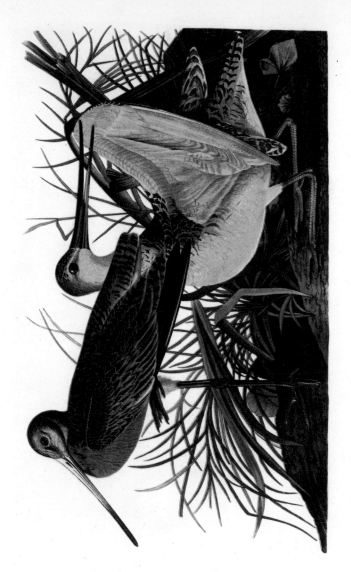

135. MARBLED GODWIT

Breeds in the wet prairies of southern Canada and the north central
states. Common in winter on the Pacific and Texas coasts, a very few
on the Atlantic. In greatly reduced numbers, once more increasing.
Length 16-20 inches.

136. HUDSONIAN GODWIT

Arctic America, migrating to southern South America, via the Texas prairies and Great Plains, a few on the Atlantic coast in fall. Reduced to the verge of extinction, now slowly increasing. Length 14-16½ inches.

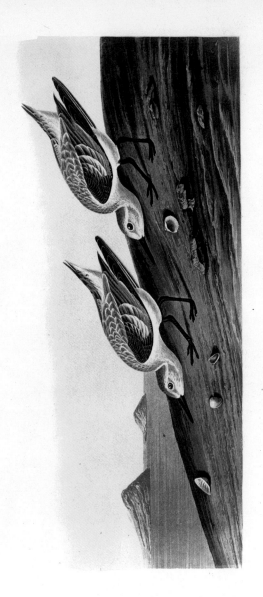

137. SANDERLING

Breeding in the Arctic, south to all continents in winter. Abundant on sandy beaches and mud flats, rare in the interior. A few winter north-ward to Cape Cod. Length 7-8½ inches.

138. AVOCET

Breeds locally in the West, east to the prairies of Canada and the central states. Sadly reduced and virtually extirpated on the Atlantic seaboard. Slowly increasing with protection. Length 16-20 inches.

139. BLACK-NECKED STILT

Tropical America north to California, Texas and Florida. After great reduction, once more common and spreading north to the Carolinas. Length 13½-15½ inches.

140. RED PHALAROPE

Arctic America, where it is common. Oceanic the rest of the year, its wintering quarters still partly unknown. Rarely seen from land in migration. Casual inland. Length 7½-9 inches.

141. WILSON'S PHALAROPE

Breeds in prairie marshes and lakes from south central Canada and the adjacent United States westward. Winters in southern South America. A few in fall on the Atlantic coast. Length 8½-10 inches.

142. POMARINE JAEGER

Arctic regions, far southward in winter. Oceanic on migration, rarely approaching outer capes and headlands. The jaegers are robbers, plundering other birds of their food. Length 20-23 inches.

143. PARASITIC JAEGER

Range and habitat exactly like the last, but much more common, a
few regularly seen from land on migration. Length 16-21 inches.

144. LONG-TAILED JAEGER

A common bird on its arctic breeding grounds, but the most pelagic
of the jaegers at other seasons. Casual near shore, and rarely seen
alive by naturalists. Length 20-23 inches.

145. ICELAND GULL

Breeds in the eastern Arctic, south in winter along the Atlantic coast
to New Jersey. The exactly similar but much larger Glaucous Gull
(26-32) occurs on the Pacific side of the Continent as well. Length
23-26 inches.

146. GREAT BLACK-BACKED GULL

Breeds from the eastern Arctic to Long Island, N. Y., a little farther
south and on the Great Lakes in winter. Rapidly increasing and
spreading southward in recent years. Length 28-31 inches.

147. HERRING GULL

Breeds from the Arctic to New Jersey and large interior lakes. Winters
south to the tropics and on the Pacific coast. Now in great abundance
in the East. Length 23-26 inches.

148. RING-BILLED GULL

Breeds in interior Canada, various central and western states. Throughout most of the United States at other seasons. Common and rapidly increasing, especially in the East. Length 18-20 inches.

149. LAUGHING GULL

Atlantic and Gulf coasts, breeding north to Nova Scotia. Greatly reduced northward in the last century, now once more common. Length 15½-17 inches.

150. BONAPARTE'S GULL

Breeds in Alaska and western Canada, wintering from the Great Lakes and New England south to the Gulf. Quite common. Sometimes nests in trees. Length 12-14 inches.

151. IVORY GULL

A rare high arctic gull, rarely straggling to the northern states in winter. Normally wintering in the Arctic on the edge of the ocean pack ice. Length 15-17 inches.

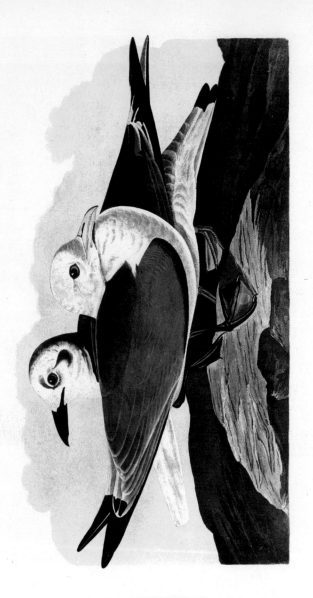

152. KITTIWAKE

Breeds in large colonies on arctic cliffs south to the Gulf of St. Lawrence. Oceanic at other seasons, rarely seen from land, and regular in
mid-ocean on steamer lanes. Length 16-18 inches.

153. COMMON TERN

Breeds on sandy beaches from southern Canada to the Gulf of Mexico,
and locally inland. Winters from south Florida to Brazil. Once more
abundant after the plume trade ceased. Length 13-16 inches.

154. ARCTIC TERN

Breeds in the Arctic south to Massachusetts. Largely oceanic at other seasons, wintering in southern oceans, and little known. Greyer than the last; bill wholly red. Common. Length 14-17 inches.

155. ROYAL TERN

Breeds on beaches from Virginia to Texas, south in winter to tropical
America. Once more increasing and quite common in the South.
Length 18-21 inches.

156. CABOT'S TERN

Rare and local from North Carolina to Texas, usually with Royal Terns.
Note the black bill with a yellow tip. Length 14-16 inches.

157. BLACK TERN

Breeds in inland marshes from Maine and Vermont through the prairies and plains to California. Migrates over the whole United States, including both coasts to South America. Very common. Length 9-10 inches.

158. BLACK SKIMMER

Coastal bays and beaches from Long Island, N. Y. to Texas. The bill
is unique in the bird world, and the long lower mandible is dipped in
the water and used as a scoop. Length 16-20 inches.

159. GREAT AUK

Perhaps the most famous of extinct birds, and the only flightless one
of North America. Formerly nested on islands in the north Atlantic,
and occurred in New England. Last specimen in 1844. Length 24
inches.

160. RAZOR-BILLED AUK

Arctic Atlantic islands south to Maine. Wintering at sea south to Long Island, usually far from land. Length 16-18 inches.

161. BRÜNNICH'S MURRE

In great colonies on cliffs and rocky islets in the north Pacific and
north Atlantic, wintering at sea often far from land. Note slender bill
compared with auk. Length 17-19 inches.

162. DOVEKIE

Breeding in great colonies in the high Arctic, wintering at sea south to Cape Hatteras. Occasionally driven ashore or inland by severe gales while migrating. Abundant. Length 7½-9 inches.

163. BLACK GUILLEMOT

Rocky shores and islets from Greenland to Maine. Wintering south to
Long Island. Not so oceanic as the other alcids, never very far from
land. Common. Length 12-14 inches.

164. MARBLED MURRELET

Pacific coast from Alaska to California. Known to breed in burrows in high mountains of Queen Charlotte Islands, but range imperfectly known. Common. Length 10 inches.

165. ATLANTIC PUFFIN

Breeds in burrows on rocky islands from Greenland to Maine. Oceanic at other seasons and little known. The bill sheath is moulted in winter, and the bill is smaller and a dull grey. Length 11½-13 inches.

166. BAND-TAILED PIGEON

Resident in the far western mountains from southern Canada to Central America. Showing some signs of increasing after a great decrease. Length 14-16 inches.

167. PASSENGER PIGEON

Formerly deciduous forests of the eastern states and southern Canada,
now extinct. One of the most abundant birds on earth, often nesting
in dense flocks of millions. Length 15-17 inches.

168. WHITE-CROWNED PIGEON

A bird of the West Indies, a very few reaching the Florida Keys as
summer breeders. Little known there since Audubon's time. Length
13½ inches.

169. MOURNING DOVE

Throughout North America from southern Canada southward except
in forested areas. Abundant, uncommon only northward where it is
migratory. Length 11-13 inches.

170. GROUND DOVE

Coastal plain and low country of the southern states from the Carolinas to Texas and far southward. Really common only in southern Texas. Length 6¾ inches.

171. CAROLINA PAROQUET

Formerly in the low country of the central and southern states east
of the Great Plains. Now extinct. Very destructive to crops, it was
mercilessly hunted as a pest. Length 13 inches.

172. YELLOW-BILLED CUCKOO

Breeds from southern Canada throughout the eastern United States,
reappearing on the Pacific slope. Winters in South America. Prefers
wood lots, copses and thickets. Length 11-12½ inches.

173. BARN OWL

Breeds in towers, old buildings, barns and hollow trees from the
central states southward. Secretive, silent, and nocturnal, it is easily
overlooked. Common only in California. Length 15-20 inches.

174. SCREECH OWL

Throughout the Continent from southern Canada southward. Now domesticated, living in city parks and suburban streets. The red phase is lacking in the West. Length 8-10 inches.

175. GREAT HORNED OWL

Locally almost throughout the New World, preferring deep woods
and swamps in the East, but often in low scrubby thickets elsewhere.
Uncommon. Length 20-23 inches.

176. SNOWY OWL

Arctic regions, south irregularly to the northern states in flights, when its food supply fails. Prefers plains, prairies, and coastal marshes and beaches. Length 20-26 inches.

177. HAWK OWL

Breeds in the northern forests of Alaska and western Canada. Rarely south in winter to the northern and eastern states. Little known. Length 15-17 inches.

178. BARRED OWL

Resident in woods and forests of the East from southern Canada to Florida and Texas. Noted for its loud hooting and its blue-black eyes. Common. Length 18-22 inches.

179. GREAT GRAY OWL

In dense northern or mountain forests of the West. Rarely south in
winter to the northern and eastern states. Not reported as common
anywhere. Length 24-33 inches.

180. LONG-EARED OWL

In woodlands from southern Canada southward. Migratory northward, and occasionally gathering in small winter flocks at roosts. Uncommon and local in the West. Length 13-16 inches.

181. RICHARDSON'S OWL

Boreal forests of Canada, southward in winter rarely and irregularly
to the northern states. Little known. Length 9-12 inches.

182. SAW-WHET OWL

Woods of southern Canada, the northern states, south in high western mountains to Mexico. Irregularly farther south in winter. So tame it can be caught alive. Length 7-8½ inches.

183. CHUCK-WILL'S-WIDOW

A bird of the southern lowland woods, a few north to the central
states. Nocturnal, insectivorous, and migrating south in winter. Common. Length 11-13 inches.

184. WHIPPOORWILL

Woodlands of southern Canada and the northern states, farther south
in the Appalachian Mountains. Reappears in the mountains of the
Southwest. Migrates to the tropics. Length 9-10 inches.

185. NIGHTHAWK

Throughout the Continent from southern Canada south in open country, plains and prairies. Is adopting flat roofs in cities. Migrating to South America in large flocks. Length 8½-10 inches.

186. CHIMNEY SWIFT

Breeding in chimneys, now very rarely in hollow trees, in eastern North America north to southern Canada. Migrating to equatorial South America. Abundant. Length 5-5½ inches.

187. ANNA'S HUMMINGBIRD

Common in gardens and woodlands in coastal California. The eastern
Ruby-throated is smaller with a shorter bill, and only the throat is red.
Length about 4 inches.

188. BELTED KINGFISHER

Widely distributed from Alaska and Labrador southward, wherever there is water containing fish and a near-by bank or bluff in which to dig its nesting burrow. Retiring southward in winter. Length 11-14 inches.

189. YELLOW-SHAFTED FLICKER

Abundant throughout eastern North America, from tree limit south.
Migratory northward. The only woodpecker which regularly feeds
on the ground. Length 13-14 inches.

190. PILEATED WOODPECKER

Resident in the forests of the East and the Rocky Mountains. Greatly reduced by lumbering in the North, now showing signs of recovery, and accepting second growth timber near mankind. Length 17-19½ inches.

191. RED-HEADED WOODPECKER

Erratically distributed in the East from southern Canada south. Rare or absent in certain areas, common in others, and local status subject to sudden change. Length 8½-9½ inches.

192. YELLOW-BELLIED SAPSUCKER

Breeds in the northern and montane evergreen forests, migrating to the southern states in winter. Only fairly common. Notably fond of sap, drilling holes for that purpose. Length 8-8½ inches.

193. DOWNY WOODPECKER

Resident in woodlands throughout the Continent from tree limit south-
ward. Tame and familiar, entering cities and suburban areas. The
Hairy Woodpecker is almost the same in color but much larger.
Length 6½-7 inches.

194. RED-COCKADED WOODPECKER

An uncommon bird peculiar to the pure pine woodlands and barrens of
the southeastern states. It is decreasing because of lumbering and
constant fires. Length 8½ inches.

195. ARCTIC THREE-TOED WOODPECKER

Resident in northern coniferous forests south to New England and
the northern Rockies. Occasionally wandering farther south in winter.
Length 9-10 inches.

196. IVORY-BILLED WOODPECKER

A magnificent woodpecker of primeval timber of the southern states,
now practically extinct chiefly from lumbering. Length 20 inches.

197. EASTERN KINGBIRD

A summer resident in open country from southern Canada southward.
Very common. Migrates to South America. Length 8½-9 inches.

198. GRAY KINGBIRD

A West Indian flycatcher, breeding locally on both coasts of Florida,
rarely to South Carolina. Note the long heavy bill. Length 9-9½ inches.

199. ACADIAN FLYCATCHER

One of a most difficult group of similar little flycatchers, best distinguished by habitat and song in the field. This one is restricted to the rich woods and swamps of the southeastern states. Length 5½-6¾ inches.

200. WOOD PEWEE

A summer resident of woodlands of the East from southern Canada south. Its sad and plaintive song attracted the attention of the early colonists. Length 6-6½ inches.

201. OLIVE-SIDED FLYCATCHER

Breeds in the northern coniferous forests, farther south in the mountains. Migrates to the tropics via Mexico, and hence rare in most of the Atlantic states. Uncommon and solitary. Length 7¼-8 inches.

202. HORNED LARK

Locally abundant from the Arctic southward in all types of dry, open,
treeless country, including beaches, plains, deserts and pastures. The
northern races are migratory, and mingle together in winter. Length
7-8 inches.

203. TREE SWALLOW

Breeds in holes in trees or nesting boxes near water from Alaska and Quebec south to the central states. Very local in the West. Abundant, gathering in enormous flocks over the marshes in fall and winter in the southern states. Length 5-6 inches.

204. TWO SWALLOWS

1. The Bank Swallow breeds locally in sand dunes, bluffs and banks throughout the Continent, wintering in South America. 2. The Violet-green Swallow breeds near cliffs in the western mountains and Pacific states south to Mexico. Uncommon.

205. BARN SWALLOW

Breeds about barns and buildings from southern Canada to the Gulf
states, migrating to South America. Ancestrally in caves and on cliffs.
Abundant in the East, less common in the West. Length 6-7½ inches.

206. CLIFF SWALLOW

Breeds from southern Canada, south locally to the central and western southern states. Attaches retort-shaped mud nests to cliffs or eaves of barns. Alleged to have invaded the East about a century ago. Length 5-6 inches.

207. PURPLE MARTIN

Breeds in bird houses, boxes and gourds from southern Canada southward, now almost completely domesticated. Local and uncommon in
the Northeast and the far West. Slowly but steadily decreasing.
Length 7½-8½ inches.

208. CANADA JAY

Breeds in late winter in the northern evergreen forests of Alaska, Canada, the northern states and high western mountains. Hardy, bold, tame, and impudent, a character of the "north woods." Length 11-12 inches.

209. BLUE JAY

Breeds in woodland and suburban estates from central Canada southward east of the Great Plains. The northern population is migratory.
Unaccountably local and rare in some sections. Length 11-12 inches.

210. FLORIDA SCRUB JAY

Locally common in scrub oak regions in peninsular Florida. Widely
separated from close relatives in California and the Southwest. A
notable case of discontinuous distribution. Length 11½ inches.

211. AMERICAN MAGPIE

Resident in western North America from Alaska to the southern Rockies. Now extending its range eastward across the Great Plains. Found in all types of country except deep forest. Length 17½-21½ inches.

212. RAVEN

Resident from Greenland and Alaska to the mountains of Nicaragua.
Preferring sea cliffs and mountains. Long since extirpated in most of
the East, where it is slowly increasing. Length 21½-26½ inches.

213. AMERICAN CROW

Breeds from central Canada south to California, Florida and Texas.
Migratory northward. Abundant in the East, uncommon and very local
in the far west, and lacking in treeless areas. Length 17-21 inches.

214. FISH CROW

Coastal marshes and low river valleys in the southern states east of the Plains, north to Rhode Island. The short, staccato nasal *caw* is readily recognizable. Length 16-20 inches.

215. BROWN-CAPPED CHICKADEE

Resident in northern evergreen forests from tree-line to the most northern states. On a few occasions wandering farther south in some numbers in winter. Length 5-5½ inches.

216. OTHER CHICKADEES

1, 2. Chestnut-backed Chickadee, in evergreen forests of the Pacific coast ranges. 3, 4. Black-capped Chickadee, common in most of Canada and the northern United States. 5, 6. Bush-tit, Pacific coast and semi-desert areas of the southern Rockies and Southwest.

217. TUFTED TITMOUSE

Resident in woodlands of the southern states north to Minnesota and
Connecticut. Has been spreading northward in recent years. Common.
Length 6-6½ inches.

218. WHITE-BREASTED NUTHATCH

In woodlands of southern Canada and most of United States. Common and well-known in most of the East, rare and local in parts of the South and West. Length 5-6 inches.

219. RED-BREASTED NUTHATCH

Breeds in the northern evergreen forests, farther south in the mountains. Migrates irregularly southward, often in great numbers, occasionally reaching the most southerly states. Length 4½ inches.

220. AMERICAN DIPPER

Mountain torrents of the West from southern Alaska to California and New Mexico. The feathers are water resistant, and it walks on the bottom of the stream. Length 7 inches.

221. HOUSE WREN

Breeds in woods, gardens and orchards from southern Canada to the
central states, wintering in the South and Mexico. Familiar and common, now rarely found in forests. Length 4½-5¼ inches.

222. TWO WRENS

1, 2, 3. Winter Wren, breeds in the northern evergreen forest belt, reaching the southern states in winter. 4. Rock Wren, resident from the western Great Plains to the Pacific in rocky places.

223. CAROLINA WREN

Resident in the southern states east of the Plains in woodland thickets
and gardens, occasionally pushing north to New England and the
Great Lakes. Common. Length. 5½-6 inches.

224. SHORT-BILLED MARSH WREN

A secretive little bird of wet, sedgy meadows from southern Canada
to the central states, wintering in the South, east of the Great Plains.
Uncommon and local. Length 4-4½ inches.

225. MOCKINGBIRD

Resident in towns, gardens, and woodland edges of the southern states, including the Southwest and California. Absent in the Great Plains. Abundant and pushing north in recent years. Length 9-11 inches.

226. CATBIRD

Breeds in woodland thickets, gardens and estates from southern Canada southward, a few in the Northwest. Winters in the South and Mexico. One of the most abundant birds in the East. Length 8½-9¼ inches.

227. BROWN THRASHER

Breeds in dry woodland thickets and scrubby hillsides from southern Canada southward east of the Rockies, wintering in the South. Common, but not domesticated like the last two members of the family. Length 10½-12 inches.

228. AMERICAN ROBIN

Breeds throughout the Continent from tree-line southward, wintering in the South. Originally a forest bird, now abundant and strictly associated with man in most of the East. Length 8½-10½ inches.

229. VEERY

Breeds from central Canada to the central states east of the Great Plains, reappearing in the Rocky Mountains. Prefers wooded swamps and moist lowland or mountain thickets. Winters in the tropics. Common. Length 6½-7½ inches.

230. BLUEBIRD

Breeds in cleared country, woodland edges, farms and gardens in tree holes or boxes, from central Canada southward, retiring southward in winter. Common and beloved in the East, local in the far West. Length 6½-7½ inches.

231. BLUE-GRAY GNATCATCHER

Breeds in woodland thickets in the more southerly states east of the Plains, retiring to the southern states and Mexico in winter. Reappears in the Southwest and California. Fairly common. Length 4½-5 inches.

232. GOLDEN-CROWNED KINGLET

Breeds in the northern evergreen forests, migrating to the southern states in winter, but some remaining in the north woods. Common. Length 3½-4 inches.

233. RUBY-CROWNED KINGLET

Slightly more northerly in breeding range than the last, south only to northern Maine. Winters in the southern states. Well known on migration in the intermediate area. Length 3¾-4½ inches.

234. CEDAR WAXWING

Breeds in woodland edges, swamp and river borders and estates from central Canada to the central states. Wintering erratically in the North and migrating to the tropics. Length 6½-8 inches.

235. BOHEMIAN WAXWING

Breeds in the evergreen forests of the far Northwest. Famous for its
erratic winter wanderings, frequently to the southern Rockies, sometimes to the Great Plains, and rarely eastward. Length 7½-8½ inches.

236. NORTHERN SHRIKE

Breeds in northern forests from tree limit to Quebec. Irregularly south
in winters, when its food supply of mice and small birds fails. Length
9-10½ inches.

237. LOGGERHEAD SHRIKE

In open or partially cleared country in the Southwest and southern states, where it is very common. North locally and uncommonly in the central states to southern Canada and western New England. Length 9 inches.

238. WARBLING VIREO

Breeds in tall shade trees in the East from southern Canada to the central states. Reappears in the West in woods and mountain forests. Decreasing in the East. Winters in the tropics. Length 5-6 inches.

239. BLACK AND WHITE WARBLER

Breeds in woodlands and forests of the East from central Canada to
the edge of the southern coastal plain. Winters in the tropics. Common
and well known. Length 5-5½ inches.

240. PROTHONOTARY WARBLER

Breeds in tree holes in the southern swamps, where it is common in the belt of cypress and gum. A few farther north. Winters in Central America. Length 5½ inches.

241. WORM-EATING WARBLER

Breeds on rich wooded hillsides in the East, in the southern and central states. Uncommon and inconspicuous. Winters in the tropics. Length 5-5½ inches.

242. TWO WARBLERS

1, 2. Golden-winged Warbler. In thickets and bushy swamps in the northern states, a small population. 3, 4. Cape May Warbler, in the eastern evergreen forests of Canada and Maine, usually rare, occasionally locally common.

243. BLUE-WINGED WARBLER

Breeds in bushy swamps and woodland edges in the central eastern states, where it is common. Hybridizes with the Golden-winged Warbler where their ranges overlap. Length 4½-5 inches.

244. ORANGE-CROWNED WARBLER

Breeds in the northern coniferous forests of Canada west of Hudson
Bay, south through the Rocky Mountains and Pacific coast ranges.
Winters in the southern states. Rare in the Northeast, common else-
where. Length 5 inches.

245. YELLOW WARBLER

Breeds in river thickets, swamp edges, gardens and estates over virtually the whole Continent. Wintering in the tropics. Very common, and relatively conspicuous for a warbler. Length 5 inches.

246. CERULEAN WARBLER

Breeds in rich deciduous woods and woodland swamps in the eastern
states west of the Alleghenies. A few local colonies on the Atlantic
coastal plain, where it is increasing. Common. Length 4-5 inches.

247. BLACKPOLL WARBLER

Breeds in northern evergreen forests from tree limit in Alaska to the higher mountains of New England and New York. Winters in South America. Very common eastward on migration, rarer westward. Length 5-5½ inches.

248. OVEN-BIRD

Breeds in woodlands and forests from central Canada to the central states. Winters in the tropics. Common in the East, more local in the Northwest. Noted for the power and volume of its song. Length 5½-6½ inches.

249. KENTUCKY WARBLER

Breeds in rich deciduous woodland thickets and swamps in the more southerly eastern states. Winters in Central America, and lacking in the Southeast. Uncommon. Length 5½ inches.

250. CONNECTICUT WARBLER

Breeds in bogs in the evergreen forests of interior Canada and the adjacent states. Winters in South America. Migrates west of the Alleghenies in spring, along the Atlantic coast in fall. Length 5¼-6 inches.

251. YELLOW-BREASTED CHAT

Breeds in bushy thickets and tangles in southern California, Texas, the
Great Plains and all but the northernmost states in the East. Secretive
and ventriloquial. Winters in Central America. Length 7-7½ inches.

252. WILSON'S WARBLER

Breeds in the northern evergreen forests from Alaska to northern
Maine, and south in the high Rocky Mountains. Migrating to Central
America, avoiding the Southeast. Common. Length 4½-5 inches.

253. REDSTART

Breeds in almost any kind of woodlands from central Canada to the southern states north of the coastal plain. In lavish abundance on migration to the tropics. Length 4½-5½ inches.

254. BOBOLINK

Breeds in fields and meadows in southern Canada, the northern and central states. Penetrating the western mountain states with irrigation and agriculture. Winters in southern South America. Length 6½-8 inches.

255. MEADOWLARK

Breeds in meadows and prairies throughout the eastern states and southern Canada. Replaced westward by the closely similar Western Meadowlark, with a different song. Length 9-11 inches.

256. THREE WESTERN ICTERIDS

1. Tricolored Blackbird, locally in marshes of interior California.
2, 3, 4. Yellow-headed Blackbird, marshes of Plains and western states.
5. Bullock's Oriole, in woods and thickets, edge of Great Plains
westward.

257. RED-WINGED BLACKBIRD

Breeds in marshes and swamps throughout North America, wintering
in the southern states. Abundant and well known. Length 7½-9½ inches.

258. BALTIMORE ORIOLE

Breeds in groves and shade-trees almost throughout the eastern states and southern Canada, meeting Bullock's Oriole on the Great Plains. Both winter in Central America. Length 7-8 inches.

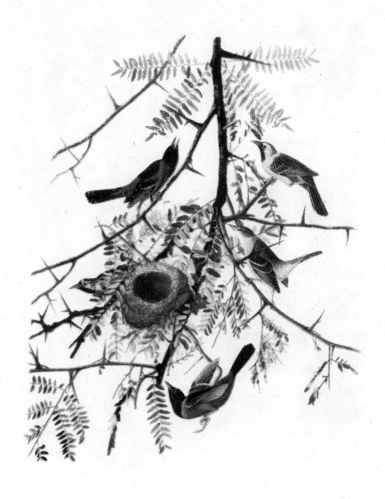

259. ORCHARD ORIOLE

Breeds in groves, thickets and orchards east of the Great Plains in all
but the most northern states. Common in the South, local and irregular
northward. Length 6-7¼ inches.

260. BOAT-TAILED GRACKLE

Outer beaches and coastal marshes from Delaware to Texas. Also inland in Florida and Texas. The two sexes are notably different in size. Length 12-17 inches.

261. PURPLE GRACKLE

Abundant in the eastern states from southern New England south to coast of Florida and Louisiana. The Bronzed Grackle ranges from Newfoundland, New England and the interior states to Texas. Length 11-13 inches.

262. COWBIRD

Almost throughout the Continent from southern Canada southward, in open country. Parasitic, laying its eggs in other birds' nests, the young raised by the foster parent. Length 7-8 inches.

263. TWO TANAGERS

1, 2. Western Tanager, in the mountain forests of the West. 3, 4. Scarlet Tanager, common in the woodlands of the East from southern Canada to the central states. Length 6½-7½ inches.

264. SUMMER TANAGER

A lovely bird of southern woodland and groves, both oak and pine
Also in the Southwest and California. Very common. All three tanagers
winter in the tropics. Length 7-7½ inches.

265. CARDINAL

Resident in thickets, tangles and gardens in the southern and south-western states north in smaller numbers through the central states to Ontario. Lacking in New England. Length 6-9 inches.

266. TWO GROSBEAKS

1. Evening Grosbeak, in northern evergreen forests and the high western mountains, irregularly southward in winter. 2, 3, 4. Black-headed Grosbeak, woodlands and forests west of the Great Plains.

267. ROSE-BREASTED GROSBEAK

Breeds in second growth woodlands of the East from southern Canada
to the central states. Wintering in the tropics. Very common. Length
7-8½ inches.

268. BLUE GROSBEAK

Breeds in brushy thickets, scrub and willow clumps from southern
California to Texas, north to Nebraska, Illinois and Maryland. Very
common southward, decreasing northward and eastward. Length
6½-7½ inches.

269. PINE GROSBEAK

Resident in northern evergreen forests from tree-line to New England
and the high western mountains. Sometimes wandering southward in
winter in great flights. Length 9-9¾ inches.

270. INDIGO BUNTING

Breeds in brushy thickets, roadsides and woodland edges from southern Canada to the Gulf states. Very common southward, irregular in the North. Winters in Central America. Length 5¼-5¾ inches.

271. PAINTED BUNTING

Breeds in brushy thickets and edges from Texas to Florida north to
Arkansas and North Carolina. Winters in south Florida and Central
America. Length 5¼ inches.

272. DICKCISSEL

Breeds chiefly in the Great Plains and prairies, sporadically east in fields to the Atlantic coast. Winters in the tropics. Abundant, but constantly shifting about for unknown reasons. Length 6-7 inches.

273. PURPLE FINCH

Breeds in northern evergreen forests from central Canada to the northern states, east of the Plains, reappearing on the Pacific coast. Erratically south in winter to the Gulf. Length 5½-6¼ inches.

274. GOLDFINCH

Breeds in woodlands, thickets, edges and gardens from central
Canada to the southern coastal plain. Migrating or wandering erratically about at other seasons. Length 5-5½ inches.

275. REDPOLL

Breeding in low thickets in the subarctic, wandering irregularly south
in winter to the central states, sometimes in great flights. Length
5-5½ inches.

276. PINE SISKIN

Breeds in northern evergreen forests, south in the high western mountains. Irregularly southward to the Gulf states, sometimes in great flights. Length 4½-5 inches.

277. RED CROSSBILL

Resident in evergreen forests northward at sea level and in nearly all
high mountain ranges. Feeds on cones almost exclusively, abandoning
any area when this crop fails. Sometimes wandering southward. Length
5¼-6½ inches.

278. THREE BUNTINGS

1. Lark Sparrow, in open fields, pastures, and prairies from the Pacific to the Alleghenies; common westward. 2, 3. Lark Bunting, in the Great Plains and western prairie bluffs. 4. Rusty Song Sparrow, northwest Pacific coast.

279. SAVANNAH SPARROW

Almost throughout the Continent in dunes, meadows and prairies, wintering in the southern states. Insignificant, but abundant. Does not breed in the South. Length 5¼-6 inches.

280. SEASIDE SPARROW

Salt marshes from Massachusetts to Florida and Texas. Secretive and
obscure, but common. A black species occurs on Merritt's Island, east
Florida, and a greenish one at Cape Sable. Length 5½-6½ inches.

281. SLATE-COLORED JUNCO

Breeds in the northern evergreen woods from Alaska to the northern states east of the Plains. Migrating south to the Gulf. Abundant, tame, a dooryard bird in winter. Length 6-6½ inches.

282. CHIPPING SPARROW

Breeds from southern Canada south to the edge of the coastal plain. Prefers farms and gardens in the East, evergreen woods or pine barrens in the West and South. Very common. Length 5-5½ inches.

283. WHITE-CROWNED SPARROW

Breeds near tree limit in northern Canada and Alaska south on the high western mountains. Wintering west of the Appalachians. Rare in the Northeast, unknown in the Southeast, abundant in the West. Length 6½-7½ inches.

284. WHITE-THROATED SPARROW

Breeds in northern evergreen forests from central Canada to the northern states east of the Plains. Floods the whole East in migration and winter. Length 6½-7 inches.

285. FOX SPARROW

Breeds in spruce thickets from tree limit in Alaska to Newfoundland, and south in the high western mountains. Floods the lowlands of both coasts and the southern states in winter. Very common. Length 6½-7½ inches.

286. SONG SPARROW

Breeds in thickets, marshes, and gardens in most of the Continent
except the extreme South. Abundant and domesticated in the East,
local and uncommon in the West. Length 5-6¾ inches.

287. LAPLAND LONGSPUR

Breeds in the Arctic. South in winter to the western plains and prairies in great flocks. A very few on the North Atlantic coast. Length 6-7 inches.

288. SNOW BUNTING

Breeds in the high Arctic. South in winter to the coastal beaches, and
the interior plains, prairies and open fields of the northern and central
states. Length 6-7¼ inches.